Spotlight on Reading

Inferring

Grades 5–6

Carson-Dellosa Publishing, LLC
Greensboro, North Carolina

Credits

Layout and Cover Design: Van Harris

Development House: The Research Masters

Cover Photo: Image Copyright mamahoohooba, 2011 Used under license from Shutterstock.com

Visit carsondellosa.com for correlations to Common Core, state, national, and Canadian provincial standards.

Carson-Dellosa Publishing, LLC
PO Box 35665
Greensboro, NC 27425 USA
carsondellosa.com

Printed in the USA • All rights reserved.   ISBN 978-1-60996-491-7
                                                              01-0032313053

About the Book

The activities in *Inferring* are designed to improve students' reading comprehension. The skill of inferring, using information to draw logical conclusions, is a higher level thinking skill—a difficult one for students to master. Inferring requires the reader to make educated guesses based on prior knowledge and on information that is implied, but not directly stated.

High-interest articles are supplemented with a variety of activities to make learning the skill of inferring fun! The exercises increase in difficulty as the book progresses, so the students practice more advanced skills as they work through the book.

With a variety of fun and instructional formats, teachers can provide direct instruction, reinforcement, or independent practice throughout the year. Have students work with partners or teams to complete the more challenging activities.

• •

Table of Contents

Prize Pumpkin

Read the poem. Use context clues to infer the answers to the questions below.

I went to the County Pumpkin Fest,
Hoping my pumpkin would be
judged best.
I lugged it all the way to the fair,
Huffing and puffing in crisp,
fresh air.
But, then I learned to my surprise,
That the judging was for pumpkin pies!

1. In what season does this poem take place? _____

   How do you know? _____

2. Do you think the speaker won the prize? _____

   How do you know? _____

3. What size was the speaker's pumpkin? _____

   How do you know? _____

4. What do you think happened next? _____

   _____

Sick Day

Look at the picture. Infer the answers to the questions below.

1. To whom is the mother talking? _____

    How do you know? _____

2. Is David really sick? _____

    How do you know? _____

3. What do you think will happen after David's mother discovers the paint?

    _____

    _____

5

Late-Night TV

Read the story. Use context clues to infer the answers to the questions below.

• •

Quinn woke up and heard strange sounds coming from the living room. She picked up her clock to check the time. It was very late!

Perplexed, she went to investigate. She discovered that the television was on—a late-night show was playing. Lying on the couch was a woman wearing a white coat. She was asleep.

Oh, Mom, Quinn thought. She must have worked late. She's always staying extra hours to help her sick patients get better.

Quinn turned off the TV. She tiptoed to Mom's side and eased her out of her white jacket. Mom did not even stir.

Quinn covered her up with an afghan and tiptoed back to bed. Soon, the whole house was quiet . . . except for the sound of snoring.

1. Is Quinn a boy or a girl? _____

   How do you know? _____

   _____

2. What does Mom do for a living? _____

   How do you know? _____

   _____

3. How does Quinn know that Mom is tired? _____

   _____

4. Does the story take place during the day or night? _____

   How do you know? _____

   _____

5. What does Quinn do at the very end of the story? _____

   How do you know? _____

   _____

First School Day

Read the story. Use context clues to infer the answers to the questions on the next page.

• •

"Rise and shine, Gregory," Mrs. Roy said as she gazed down at the lump in the bed. "Today is a big day!"

The lump did not move. Mrs. Roy leaned over and shook the bed. A groan came from beneath the covers. Gregory rolled out from under them.

Mrs. Roy approached the second bed. "Wake up, Christopher! Summer is over. No more sleeping late." A head slowly peeked out, followed by the rest of a disheveled body.

"Be downstairs in ten minutes," the boys' mother instructed. She left the room.

Gregory went into the bathroom and turned on the water. "Thith will be a thuper year," he said. A toothbrush extended from his mouth.

"What?" Christopher asked. He changed out of his pajamas and into blue jeans. He heard Gregory spit into the sink.

"I said 'this will be a super year,'" Gregory repeated. "New classes, new teachers, and a junior basketball team!" He winked.

Christopher looked a bit less confident. "I'm pretty nervous," he admitted. "I'm new at this, you know."

"Oh, middle school takes a little getting used to," Gregory agreed. "But after a few days it will feel like you've been there forever! Remember, I had to go through it last year."

"Now, you're a BIG seventh grader and practically run the school," Christopher teased.

"Just don't do anything to ruin my reputation," Gregory warned, smiling back.

"You mean like tell everyone how you think Jenny Page is the prettiest girl in the school? "

Gregory blushed. Just then, some wonderful smells wafted into the room. Both boys halted and inhaled deeply.

"Race you downstairs!" Gregory shouted. The boys ran off to start the new year.

7

First School Day (cont.)

Write the answers on the lines.

• •

1. How do the boys feel about waking up early? _____

_____

2. What makes this a "big day"?_____

_____

3. Describe the boys' relationship to each other. _____

_____

4. At what time of day does this episode take place?_____

_____

5. Why is Gregory difficult to understand when he first speaks? _____

_____

6. What grade is Christopher entering?_____

7. How does each boy feel about the upcoming year?

Gregory: _____

_____

Christopher: _____

_____

8. What is waiting for the boys downstairs? _____

8 Inferring • CD-104555

⭐ Mystery of the Smudged Words

Read the story. Look at the message. Use context clues to infer the answers to the questions below.

• •

Amy came in from playing outside and opened a letter from her pen pal. Her fingers were sweaty, and some of the ink from the page got on her hands.

Amy peered closely at the letter. There were several smudges on it. Amy couldn't make out all of the words. She mentioned the problem to her mother.

"Mom," Amy said, "I can't figure out what these three words are. They're covered with a purple stain."

"Use the context to help you," Amy's mother suggested.

"What do you mean?" Amy inquired.

"The context includes the things surrounding what you are looking for," her mother said. "Look at the words around it. They will give you some clues."

"So, context clues are things that help you figure something out," Amy responded.

"Exactly!" her mother replied, beaming.

"I feel like a detective," Amy said proudly. "I'll try to solve the mystery of the purple-smudged words!"

Dear Amy,
  Thanks for ~~smudged~~ me back so quickly! I enjoyed your letter. It's a sunny afternoon in Phoenix. I'm out on the deck of my swimming ~~smudged~~ getting a suntan. Soon, I'll go for a dip. But first, I'll finish this yummy peanut-butter and ~~smudged~~ sandwich and wait a half-hour. Mom says I should wait after eating. Mothers! They sure have a lot of rules! Well, I hope to hear from you soon!
                                    Yours truly,
                                    Debbie

---

1. What is the first smudged word? _____
   What are the clues? _____

2. What is the second smudged word? _____
   What are the clues? _____

3. What is the third smudged word? _____
   What are the clues? _____

To The Moon!

Read the paragraph. Use context clues to infer the meaning of the words in **bold**. Circle the answers to the questions below.

• •

When astronauts explored the moon in the late 1960s and early 1970s, they collected samples of moon rocks for scientists to study. It was difficult to **trek** across the rough **lunar** surface. It was even hard to **haul** all of the samples back to the Lunar Module, not because they were heavy, but because they were **bulky**. The astronauts needed some kind of vehicle. NASA invented a car for them. It was called the Lunar **Rover** or Moon Buggy.

1. The word trek means. . .
   a. ride.
   b. hike.
   c. dance.

2. The word lunar relates to . . .
   a. the stars.
   b. the sun.
   c. the moon.

3. The word haul means. . .
   a. walk.
   b. carry.
   c. play.

4. The word rover means . . .
   a. traveler.
   b. builder.
   c. worker.

5. The word bulky means . . .
   a. tiny.
   b. blue.
   c. large.

Try this: Fill in the missing word. Smooth is to rough as bulky is to _____.

        tiny   carry   compact

Final Exam

Mrs. Lindsey's class had their final exam on Monday. Not everyone studied for it, though. Look at the pictures. Use context clues to infer the answers to the questions on the next page.

Final Exam (cont.)

Circle or write the correct answers.

. . . .

1. On Sunday, the boy...

    studied   did not study

    When the test was given on Monday, he felt . . .

    confident   nervous

    . . . because he

    was prepared   was not prepared

2. What grade do you think he received? _____

3. On Sunday, the girl . . .

    studied   did not study

    When the test was given on Monday, she felt...

    confident   nervous

    . . . because she

    was prepared   was not prepared

4. What grade do you think she received? _____

     Inferring • CD-104555

Name _____

Read the clues. Infer the name of the object the clues describe. Write the name on the line.

1. Some people collect me.
   People stick me on packages.
   Without me, you wouldn't receive your birthday cards!
   I am a _____.

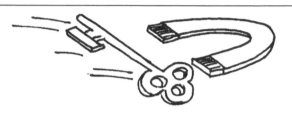

2. Objects made of metal cling to me.
   I have a north pole and a south pole.
   I can stick to refrigerators.
   I am a _____.

3. I am a narrow, flexible strip
   I protect wounds from bacteria.
   I stick to skin but not cuts.
   I am a _____.

4. I am a ball of hot gas.
   Astronomers study me.
   I burn brightly in the sky.
   I am a _____.

5. I am a source of bright light.
   You use me indoors.
   I contain a wire filament.
   I am a _____.

6. I am a bright flash of light in the sky.
   You'll see me when it's wet outside.
   Thunder usually follows me.
   I am _____.

The Big Concert

Look at the illustrations. Infer what is happening. Write a sentence to describe what the girl wants in each frame.

Example: Frame #1
The girl wants <u>to go to the concert</u>.

1. Frame #2
    The girl wants _____.

2. Frame #3
    The girl wants _____.

3. Frame #4 and #5
    The girl wants _____.

An Inference Incident

Read the story. Use context clues to infer the answers to the questions on the next page.

• •

"Quiet down, students. Go back to your desks," Mr. Chan said. He waited for everyone to get settled. "Please take out your writing journals. Today we will be learning about inference."

"Is that like a conference?" Daphne asked eagerly. The students often held conferences to discuss their stories, and Daphne had just finished a good one.

"No," replied Mr. Chan. "But that's a good guess. In fact, that's what inference is—making an educated guess based on what you already know. Daphne saw that we were using our journals and inferred that we would be doing something that involved writing. Good job, Daphne!"

Just then, a loud clang rang through the room. The students put down their materials and lined up at the door. They walked single file out to the playground. They whispered in excitement when a red truck with a ladder on top drove up to the school. Men and women carried a water hose around to the side of the building. A small puff of smoke blew out of a window near the school's cafeteria.

"Don't worry," Mr. Chan reassured them. "Everyone is safe. The situation will be taken care of shortly. However, I'm going to make an inference. I infer that we may be eating lunch in our classroom today instead of in the cafeteria!"

15

An Inference Incident (cont.)

Circle the correct answers. Write down the clues that helped you figure them out.

• •

1. At the beginning of the article, the students are . . .
    a. quietly working on an assignment.
    b. out of their desks and making noise.
    c. working on a science experiment.
    How do you know? _____

2. Daphne feels _____ her finished story.
    a. proud and excited to share
    b. dissatisfied with
    c. ashamed of
    How do you know? _____

3. The clang is . . .
    a. the children misbehaving.
    b. a fire alarm.
    c. a thunderstorm.
    How do you know? _____

4. The people who arrive at the school are . . .
    a. police officers.
    b. firefighters.
    c. a TV crew.
    How do you know? _____

5. The smoke is most likely caused by . . .
    a. burnt pizza.
    b. a science experiment.
    c. library books burning.
    How do you know? _____

Save the Day

Read the story. Use context clues to infer the answers to the questions on the next page.

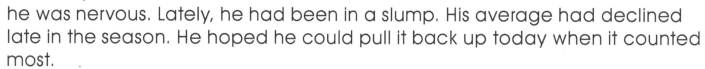

Tate raced toward the baseball diamond. He greeted his teammates, jumping up and down. "Are you ready to win the championship?" he asked.

His two best friends, Jeffrey and Amira, smiled at his excitement. "It looks like our star batter is ready," Jeffrey said.

Jeffrey did not want to admit that he was nervous. Lately, he had been in a slump. His average had declined late in the season. He hoped he could pull it back up today when it counted most.

Amira was calm, as usual. She never seemed to get butterflies in her stomach, even under pressure. She was the team's pitcher and had a mean fastball.

The players warmed up and took the field. The game was a close one, but Tate and his team were victorious in the end. Afterward, the three buddies went to an ice cream shop to celebrate.

"Great job today, Amira!" Tate complimented his friend. "You kept your cool even when we were behind 2 to 0."

"Thanks." Amira said. She licked at her black raspberry ice cream. Not a drip escaped off the cone.

"You were great, too!" Tate said to Jeffrey. "When you hit that ball over the fence in the fifth inning, I almost knocked the bench over while cheering!"

The two boys gave each other high fives. In their enthusiasm, the boys knocked Tate's ice cream off its cone.

"Oh, no," Tate said.

"Sorry, Tate," Jeffrey said. But Jeffrey could not stop smiling. He was in too good a mood. He'd hit the winning run today, and he felt great. He hadn't let his team down. Now, he would not let his friend down.

"I have some money left," he said to Tate. "Let's go back up to the counter, so I can save the day again!"

1. How does Tate feel before the game? _____

   How do you know? _____

   _____

2. Do you think Tate played well in the game? _____

   How do you know? _____

   _____

3. How does Jeffrey feel before the game? _____

   How do you know? _____

   _____

4. Do you think Jeffrey played well in the game? _____

   How do you know? _____

   _____

5. How does Amira feel before the game? _____

   How do you know? _____

   _____

6. Do you think Amira played well in the game? _____

   How do you know? _____

   _____

Most Valuable Player

Read the story and look at the picture. Identify how Mona feels. Write a letter to a friend with clues that help them infer how Mona feels.

• •

Mona had sweaty hands as she gripped the bat. This was the last inning of the game, and the score was still tied. She stepped up to the plate and waited for the pitcher to throw the ball.

The ball came fast. Mona swung. She hit the ball so hard it flew into the air and over the fence. A home run!

Dear _____ ,

_____

_____

_____

_____

_____

_____

_____

_____

_____

_____

What were your context clues? List them here:

1. _____
2. _____
3. _____

19

A Very Rainy Day

Read the story and answer the questions on the next page.

• •

The winds had finally died down, and the rains had stopped. Paige and her parents were inside their house, sitting in the living room, which was dark except for a single candlelight.

"Let's find out what's going on outside," Paige's mom suggested as she turned on the small radio.

" . . . has moved out of the area," an announcer's voice boomed. "Winds reaching nearly 100 miles an hour passed through our town this morning. But, the worst is over, and it is now safe to go outside. Suddenly, the radio went dead. The house was quiet again.

"Well," Paige's dad said, optimistically, "at least we heard some good news, even if it was cut short. Let's look out the window and survey the damage."

Paige raced to the window and peered outside. She saw tree branches strewn across the lawn. The mailbox was bent at a crazy angle, and some of the address letters and numbers on the mailbox were missing.

"The wind must have ripped them off," Paige's father noted. As he read the remaining letters he began to chuckle. Paige and her mom joined in the mirth.

The mailbox displayed
_____ _____R _____ AIN.

A Very Rainy Day (cont.)

Circle the correct answer.

1. The weather event that took place that day was . . .

   a. an earthquake.   b. a hurricane.   c. a flood.

2. The living room was dark because . . .

   a. there were no lamps.

   b. someone forgot to pay the electric bill.

   c. the electricity had been knocked out.

3. The radio they were using was . . .

   a. battery-powered.   b. electric.   c. a short-wave radio.

4. The radio went off because . . .

   a. it was turned off by Paige.

   b. the batteries died.

   c. there was nothing left to say.

5. In this context, the word survey means to . . .

   a. evaluate the situation.   b. clean up.   c. make.

6. The family's name could have been . . .

   a. Main.   b. Crain.   c. Germain.

7. After the storm had passed, Paige's family felt . . .

   a. relieved.   b. disappointed.   c. scared.

Try this: Write a story about a family that lives through another type of severe weather event.

Name _____

Read the story. Look at the weather forecast on the next page. Use context clues to infer the answers to the questions.

• •

The alarm clock blared its disturbingly cheerful tune. Chase Foster groaned as he pried open his eyelids—and wheezed. He reached for the inhaler on the nightstand and took a puff. Chase sighed as he rose and padded to the living room.

"How are you feeling this morning?" his mother asked. "Are you having trouble breathing?"

"I feel terrific, Mom. I've never felt better."

His mother looked doubtful. "Tonight's soccer game has been cancelled due to poor air quality."

"Are you sure?"

She nodded. "This drought has lasted for weeks, and there isn't the slightest breeze to blow the pollution away."

Winsome Valley was a great place to live. Citizens looked out for one another, businesses thrived, and the population grew at a steady but manageable rate. No community was finer—unless it did not rain.

Without precipitation or a good breeze to keep them from settling, particulates hovered over Winsome Valley like a sallow, greasy fog. Dust, pollen, smoke, and car exhaust blanketed the valley. Healthy people experienced stinging eyes and coughs. People with illnesses like asthma faced serious breathing problems

"What does the weather forecast predict?" asked Chase.

His mother stroked his hair and smiled. "Your heart is set on this camping trip, isn't it?"

"We're going to go canoeing and horseback riding. It's our last chance before school starts." Chase gave his mother his saddest expression.

"You can't go if the air quality is bad, Chase."

Chase sighed. He felt disappointed because he was so excited to camp.

She must have noticed because she patted his shoulder and said in a sympathetic tone, "Weather is changeable, Chase. Don't give up hope. All we need is a little rain or a steady breeze. On Friday, you should be heading to Winsome Valley State Park."

Bad Air Blues (cont.)

Circle or write the correct answer.

• •

National Weather Service Five-Day Forecast for Winsome Valley:

Wednesday	**Thursday**	**Friday**	**Saturday**	**Sunday**
Chance of rain: 80%	Chance of Rain: 90%	Chance of rain: 60%	Chance of rain: 40%	Chance of rain: 40%
Mild winds from the north	Strong winds from the north	Mild winds from the north	Mild winds from the east	Breezy winds from the east

  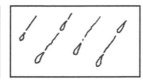  

1. What condition does Chase have?
   A. He has a cold.
   B. He has asthma.
   C. He has a sprained ankle.

2. If the weather forecast is accurate, will Chase go camping? _____
   How do you know? _____

3. Write an ending for the story.

   _____
   _____
   _____
   _____

The Disappearing Backpack

Read the story. Use context clues to infer the answers to the questions below.

• •

Robin and her brother Theo were walking to the school bus stop when their pet dog dashed by.

"Kramer has escaped!" Robin shouted.

Theo put his backpack on a trash can at the end of a nearby driveway. He chased after Kramer, managing to grab the canine by the collar. While he struggled to keep Kramer in his grasp, his father ran up the street with a leash.

"He got away from me," Dad explained. He marched Kramer back home.

When Theo went to retrieve his backpack, it was nowhere to be found. He noticed a large truck driving away in the distance. A look of panic crossed Theo's face. He peered into the empty trash can, then raced down the street after the vehicle.

1. What probably happened to Theo's backpack? _____

    _____

2. What clues led you to that conclusion? _____

    _____

Robin deduced what had happened to Theo's backpack. While Theo chased after the truck, Robin ran and caught up with her father. She explained the situation. Her dad promised to make some phone calls as soon as he arrived home.

Two hours later, while Theo was sitting in his classroom, there was a knock on the door. A student messenger entered. The student was carrying Theo's backpack!

"Special delivery from the main office," the student smiled. "Or should I say, smelly *delivery*!"

Theo was overjoyed. His books were unharmed. But, they certainly did have a distinct odor!

3. Whom did the father call? _____

4. What does the student messenger mean by smelly delivery? _____

    _____

5. How might Theo's classmates feel about sitting near him that day? _____

    _____

Name _____

The Audition

Read the story. Use context clues to infer the answers to the questions on the next page.

. . . .

Hayley's heart thudded as she took her place in the registration line. When she reached the front, a woman handed her an application. Hayley completed it, leaving the section marked *Experience* empty.

Applicants crowded the lobby—discussing, laughing, and stretching their muscles. Some girls wore dance attire. Hayley felt awkward in her simple T-shirt and shorts. Her stomach twisted from nerves.

She nearly vaulted out of her seat when someone tapped on her shoulder. "Hi, Hayley! Trying out for the production?"

Hayley nodded. She recognized the girl as Roxanne from geography class.

"The dance portion of the audition will be difficult in those flip-flops. Did you bring a pair of character shoes?

"What are character shoes? Hayley asked.

Roxanne smiled sympathetically. "I have an extra pair of jazz sneakers in my backpack. They are flexible, and I think they will fit."

"Thank you. I must have *amateur* emblazoned on my forehead. I probably shouldn't audition, but I love singing."

Roxanne's grin lit up her face. "We are all amateurs, and it is fantastic! The choreographer will conduct the dance audition after the vocal audition. I looked at the schedule. You audition right before me! Have you marked 16 bars on your music?"

"What do you mean by 16 bars?"

Roxanne reached for the sheet music in Hayley's hand. "You need to sing 16 measures of music from your audition piece. If the director likes your voice, he might ask you to sing more. You should try these ones." Roxanne marked the page and tilted her head. "They just called your number!"

Hayley checked the paper in front of her. She gulped.

"Break a leg," Roxanne said.

"What?"

"It means 'good luck!'" Roxanne pushed Hayley up to the stage.

Hayley's legs were shaking so hard she wondered if they would shatter. She handed her sheet music to the accompanist, but she was nervous about singing with a piano. She'd never done it before. Luckily, after a couple of bars she lost herself in the music. She almost forgot to stop!

The Audition (cont.)

A man in the audience clapped. "That was very nice. Would you please sing a little more?"

Hayley grinned. "Absolutely!"

1. Is this Hayley's first time auditioning for a show? _____

    How do you know? _____

    _____

2. Has Hayley had dance training? _____

    How do you know? _____

    _____

3. How does Hayley feel about the audition? _____

    How do you know? _____

    _____

4. Does Hayley have a good chance for a part? _____

    How do you know? _____

    _____

Inferring • CD-104555

Snowman Life Cycle

Read the story. Use context clues to infer the answers to the questions on the next page.

• •

Sydney and Denis shivered and zipped up their jackets as they left their grandmother's house after their usual Friday visit. The sky was a dark gray, with big clouds blocking the pale winter sun. The two siblings arrived home to find the trees on their lawn swaying back and forth. That night, the windows whistled and shook in their frames, making it difficult to sleep.

Sydney and Denis woke up Saturday morning to a world of whiteness against a backdrop of clear blue. It looked as if some mad baker had sprinkled powdered sugar all over their neighborhood. They celebrated by building a gigantic snowman and having a snowball fight. That evening, they warmed themselves by a crackling fire.

After lunch on Sunday, Sydney and Denis scrambled to see their snowman. They laughed at the sight of his deformed features. The snowman's button eyes had slipped down to his chin, and his carrot nose protruded through his throat.

As they left for school on Monday, there was no new snow, but snow that had melted Sunday had become ice. The snowman's face was frozen. The button eyes remained in their awkward position, and the icy carrot stayed tightly lodged, glistening in the early morning sun.

After school, they ran outside without jackets to visit their snowman. They giggled at his shrunken head. They tried to patch him up, but it was a losing battle. The poor snowman's body looked even more lopsided than ever!

Tuesday afternoon, the kids grabbed umbrellas and hurried to the see the snowman. Sydney and Denis stared forlornly at the remains. The snowman was a small pile of wet snow now. Some creature had gnawed on the carrot nose. Denis's boots squished as he picked up the black buttons that had once been eyes. His gloves were soaked from the task. He and Sydney trudged back to the house.

That evening, the siblings cheered up while watching the local news on TV. The weather forecast was predicting another cold front, with several inches of snow to follow on the weekend. They could rebuild. This time, they decided, it would be a snow woman, and according to the weather report, she would survive for quite a while.

Snowman Life Cycle (cont.)

Use the weather forecasts provided to fill in the blanks.

sunny

Word Bank

cool and clear

windy and snowy

cold and clear

cool and rainy

rain

1. Friday night it is _____.

2. Saturday morning it is _____.

3. Sunday afternoon it is _____.

4. Sunday night it is _____.

5. Monday afternoon it is _____.

6. Tuesday afternoon it is _____.

snow

cold front

In the Cellar

Read the story. Use context clues to infer the answers to the questions below.

• •

Abigail opened the cellar door. It groaned on rusty hinges. Although it was still bright outside, the cellar was shadowy. Carrying a lantern in one hand and a basket of food in the other, she carefully went downstairs. When she reached the bottom, she whispered, "I brought you some supper."

She raised the lantern and surveyed the room. Three dark figures crouched among the boxes and barrels. She heard a soft whimper from the smallest figure. "Do not be afraid. I am a friend with friends."

As her eyes adjusted to the darkness, she could see a family—a man, a woman, and a little girl. The three journeyed north on the secret route known as the Underground Railroad.

"Passengers" traveled from station to station in secret, usually at night, hidden in crates, bags, or boxes. "Conductors" were their guides, leading them to the next station, the next safe haven on their road to freedom. Conductors would announce themselves as "a friend with friends."

The road to freedom was treacherous for passengers, conductors, and stationmasters. The danger came from soldiers, federal marshals, and even neighbors. If caught, Abigail's father would be imprisoned. "No price is too high for liberty," he always said.

Abigail noticed that the girl was shivering. Abigail ran up the stairs, straight to her bedroom. She found her favorite doll, Liberty, resting on the bedcovers. She picked up the doll, hugged it tightly, and then ran back to the cellar. The little girl was still trembling.

Abigail handed her the doll. "This is Liberty. When I am afraid at night, I hold her close, and I feel brave. I want you to have her."

The girl took the doll and hugged it close. Her father and mother smiled at Abigail. As she ascended the stairs, she said to the girl, "Take good care of her. Liberty is a precious thing."

1. During which war does this story take place? _____

2. What clue tells you there is a war?_____

_____

3. From what is the family in the cellar trying to escape? _____

Land! Land!

Read the story. Use context clues to infer the answers to the questions on the next page.

Juan was a crew member on a large sailing vessel, one of three bound for the Indies. His job was to feed the crew. However, after a few months of sailing, the patience of the crew was wearing thin. They had been cooped up for some time with no sign of their destination. The food didn't help. Without making port, they couldn't stock up on new foods.

"Dried meat, again?" Charles complained as Juan served his meal. Charles missed fresh foods and was suffering from scurvy, a disease caused by a lack of vitamin C.

"I miss my wife," Tomás moaned. "And my friends. Sometimes I wish we'd just turn the ship around!"

"Be strong, gentlemen," Juan told them. "Our fine captain will steer us to the land of spices."

"You're right," Charles said, grudgingly. "He's a smart man, that Cristóbal!"

Juan had faith that the ship would soon reach land. When the voyage was over, he would have exciting tales to tell. But for now, he had to deal with his disgruntled shipmates. He portioned out their scanty rations.

That night, Juan was awakened from a restless sleep by a loud shout.

"Land! Land!" he heard as he joined the other sleepy men on deck. An audible sigh came from the crew. It was true. Land was visible in the distance. Who could guess what might be in store for them now?

Land! Land! (cont.)

1. In what year might this story have taken place? _____

2. Who do you think was the ship's captain? _____
    What are the clues? _____
    _____

3. Why was the food so bad? _____

4. What is the meaning of the word scanty? _____

5. Where did the ship land? _____

6. Write a few sentences describing what happened after the story. (What did Juan see? How did he feel?) _____
    _____
    _____
    _____
    _____
    _____

Classroom Trial

Read the story. Use context clues to infer the answers to the questions below.

Mrs. Hirsch's sixth-grade class was holding a mock trial. The plaintiff was Nassim, who claimed Zachary had taken his pen. The jury members were the students. They were prepared to hear each boy's testimony.

"It's my pen," Nassim insisted. "My uncle, who is an astronaut, gave it to me. It writes upside down and can be used in outer space. It also writes in a variety of colors."

"It's my pen," Zachary said. "Ask my brother." Some of the students glanced at each other. They knew that Zachary's brother was only one year old. He did not know what a pen was.

Mrs. Hirsch passed around Exhibit A. It was a writing utensil that had the words "NASA Space Program" printed along the side.

The boys left the room while the class deliberated the facts of the case.

An hour later, Zachary was cleaning the chalkboards and scowling. His face was red. Nassim was at his desk, writing a story. He beamed contentedly.

1. Do you believe the plaintiff or the defendant? _____

2. What evidence leads you to your conclusion? _____

   _____

3. Name one thing Nassim said that helped prove his case. _____

   _____

4. Explain how each boy felt at the end of the story and why.
   a. Nassim _____

   _____

   b. Zachary _____

   _____

Wildlife Rescue

Read the story. Use context clues to infer the answers to the questions below.

• •

Umberto spied something small wriggling on the ground. At first, he thought it was a frog or a mouse, but when he took a closer look, he saw it was a baby bird. Umberto ran inside to call the wildlife rehabilitation center.

"If the baby bird looks hurt, you need to bring it to the rehabilitation center," said the woman. "If he is not hurt, you need to determine his level of development. If he has feathers, he is what we call a fledgling. Fledglings are supposed to hop around on the ground. If the bird is in a safe place, leave it alone. If it isn't safe, pick it up and put it in a nearby bush or tree. Its parents are probably close."

"It's ok for me to touch it?" Umberto asked. "Won't the parents ignore it or hurt it if they smell my scent on the baby?"

"Most birds don't have a strong sense of smell. The parents won't reject it. If you need to touch the baby to make it safe, go ahead," she said. "If the baby bird does not have feathers or is fuzzy, it is called a nestling. If you see a nest that you can reach safely, put the baby in the nest. If the nest is missing, you can make a substitute nest from a basket. Fill the nest with dried leaves or pine straw. Create an indentation in the center of the material and place the baby bird there. Hang it in a tree close to where you found the baby. In either case, watch the nest for a couple of hours, and if the parents do not return, bring the baby to the center."

Umberto thanked the woman and ran back to the baby bird. He picked it up and inspected it. He examined the tree under which he found it. He ran back to the house and returned with his father and a ladder. His father held the ladder still while Umberto placed the baby bird back into its nest. He checked on the baby a couple of hours later, and satisfied, he rode to the park.

1. Was the baby bird a fledgling or a nestling? What is your evidence?

    _____

2. Was the baby bird injured? What is your evidence? _____

    _____

3. Did the parents return? What is your evidence? _____

    _____

Sitia and Exultation

Read the story. Use context clues to infer the answers to the questions on the next page.

• •

A cool breeze blowing across the rooftop woke Sitia just before dawn. Soon Khepri would emerge from behind Bakhu, the eastern mountain, and push the sun across the arched body of Nut, the goddess of the sky. Sitia had watched beetles form ox dung and roll it across the courtyard behind their house many times. He had no trouble imagining the god with a scarab's head pushing the disk of the sun.

Now it was dark. Everyone else was asleep. Sitia could see their shadowy forms in the starlight. He put his hands behind his head and gazed up at the glittering sky. An unmistakable line of stars lay on the horizon. At this quiet hour even he, a potter's son, could gaze upon the great Osiris, the god in whom all Pharaohs dwelled. Even the smallest child knew that the great builders of pyramids came from Osiris, ruled on Earth for a while, then returned to the starry body in the heavens.

There was nothing wrong with being the son of Tia, the potter. The god who fashioned the souls of all men was a potter. Still, sometimes, the son of Tia, Sitia, wished to be important. He wanted someone, anyone, to listen to him. He wanted someone to jump to his bidding, just once, as he always had to for his father, his mother, customers, and even strangers in the street.

He closed his eyes and fell asleep. When he woke again, the sun was high. His older brother was shaking him. "What is wrong?" he asked. "Father and Uncle Ahmose are waiting for you," his brother answered.

Sitia hurried down to the pottery shop. Like many families of tradesmen in their town, they lived in rooms above their father's place of business. When he saw his uncle, Sitia froze. The older man was holding a puppy in his arms.

"I have a favor to ask of you, Sitia," he said. "The master at the great house has many hunting dogs. This morning he told me he had too many. He wanted me to take this one home with me," Ahmose paused. "It was a great honor, but I could not. My wife, as you know, has a miu." He shook his head. "How she spoils that cat. I had to buy it a new earring just last week."

"Our cat was the same. We paid the price, but it was worth it. We shall meet again in the next life," Sitia's father said.

Sitia and Exultation (cont.)

Circle the correct answers.

"Sitia, you once told me that you wanted someone to listen to you." Ahmose continued. "This iwiw will listen well." He handed the little dog to Sitia. As the young iwiw licked his face, Sitia was overwhelmed.

"I shall call him Exultation," Sitia said. "My Uncle, you do listen to the voice of my heart. The happiness of that knowledge shall follow me as surely as this wondrous companion."

1. This story takes place . . .

    a. in the past.   b. in the present.   c. in the future.

2. This story takes place in . . .

    a. Egypt.   b. Hawaii.   c. France.

3. What is the genre?

    a. non-fiction   b. folk tale   c. biography

4. When it was warm, families slept . . .

    a. on the ground.   b. on the roof.   c. in the shop.

5. When Sitia grew up he was going to be . . .

    a. a Pharaoh.   b. a weaver.   c. a potter.

6. Ahmose worked for . . .

    a. a weaver.   b. a rich man.   c. Sitia's father.

7. What is a "miu"?

    a. a horse   b. a mouse   c. a cat

8. Cats sometimes wore . . .

    a. hats.   b. jewelry.   c. shoes.

9. What is an iwiw?

    a. a dog   b. a cat   c. a monkey

Name _____

Read the story. Use context clues to infer the answers to the questions below. Circle or write the correct answers.

• •

"Come on, Mom!" Peter urged. He practically dragged her through the revolving front doors. They made their way toward a room with a sign that read "Department of Motor Vehicles."

Once inside the room, Peter completed some paperwork. Then he joined a long line of people. They were waiting their turn at the counter. As Peter waited, he stared at a poster on the wall. It read, "You must be at least 16 to apply for a license."

As Peter moved forward, he peppered his mom with questions. "You'll let me have the keys right away, won't you?" he asked. "It's all right if I take it out tonight, isn't it? I'll fill up the tank, I promise."

An hour later, Peter raced out of the building with a huge grin on his face. His success was evident. "Come on, Mom!" he called. "Your driver is ready to take you home!"

1. When Peter first enters the building, he feels . . .

    a. agitated.   b. relieved.   c. impatient.

2. Where is Peter? Why is Peter here? _____

    _____

    List three clues that help you come to that conclusion.

    a. _____

    b. _____

    c. _____

3. The word peppered as used in this reading selection means to . . .

    a. ask.   b. spice.   c. shower with.

4. To what keys is Peter referring? _____

5. What tank is he talking about? _____

6. Describe how Peter felt upon leaving the building, and why. _____

    _____

    _____

Name _____

Save the Elephants

Read the story. Use context clues to infer the answers to the questions below.

• •

During the 1980s, the African elephant population declined. Originally, there were one million elephants, but this number went as low as 600,000 animals. The African elephant was in a threatening situation; it would soon be an endangered species!

Thankfully there were people concerned about elephant welfare. They created organizations to protect animals, especially elephants. They devised a plan to alleviate the situation. They began a publicity campaign to spread awareness of the problem.

One big cause of the declining elephant population was the ivory industry. Ivory had to be harvested from elephants before being sold. Some large companies helped fix the problem by refusing to buy ivory and asking their customers to do the same.

International laws were eventually passed to make ivory illegal around the world. Since they could not sell ivory, people stopped bothering the elephants.

1. What do you think would have happened to the African elephant if no one had made any changes? _____

    Why? _____

    _____

2. What do you think will happen in the future now that elephants are protected? _____

    Why? _____

    _____

Where Are They?

Use context clues below to figure out where each location is. Write the name of the place.

• •

1. Kristin and Larry are browsing through the stacks. They accidentally bump into each other. Volumes tumble with a crash. A man behind a desk puts his index finger to his lips in warning.

    Location: _____

2. The crew has been confined underwater for months. The sonar has not picked up anything unusual, so the tour of duty has been uneventful. Suddenly, the crew feels a large jolt. Crew members rush to the periscope to see what hit them.

    Location: _____

3. Floating and weightless, the men and women maneuver around each other, manning controls and performing duties while the earth and stars appear brightly as a backdrop.

    Location: _____

4. The stalactites glowed iridescently in the dark, providing an eerie environment for the adventurous explorers. Bats hung from the ceiling above.

    Location: _____

5. The boys stepped cautiously with their bare feet in the thick mud. The air was very humid and heavy. Trees and strange plants blocked out the sun overhead. Rain drops pinged off the leaves. Any minute, the boys expected to find the largest snake in the world.

    Location: _____

6. We are traveling at break-neck speed with a monotonous clickety-clack ringing in our ears. Steam flies out of the engine and past the windows. The conductor comes to take our tickets, while the engineer pulls the whistle. Choo! Choo!

    Location: _____

A Surprise for Krysia

Read the story. Use context clues to infer the answers to the questions on the next page.

• •

Magda Banas waved to Krysia from across the crowded dirt street. "Come," she called. "I have something to show you."

Krysia looked back at the dilapidated apartment building. Her four brothers were still at the factory and her mother, in their tiny room on the second floor, was busy mending clothes. Krysia knew that nobody would miss her if she did not stay away too long. She dodged two delivery wagons and a buggy to catch up with her friend. One of the horses whinnied and snorted at her.

"What is it?" she asked in Polish.

"Speak only English. I want to learn," her friend said. She was already hurrying down the street, dodging men and women in dark, tattered clothes who chattered to each other in five different languages.

"Where are we going?" Krysia asked, breathless.

"I cannot tell you. I want it to be—how do they say—a surprise. Come." She cut down an alley between two tenements.

A woman was hanging out her laundry on a line above them. She waved. "Where are you girls going?" she asked.

"To the Settlement House," Magda called.

"Oh, yes! I have been there. That Miss Jane Addams is an angel," the woman said.

"What is the Settlement House?" Krysia asked.

"You will see," Magda said. "We are almost there."

They stepped out of the alley, crossed another street and stood in front of a large brick house. Krysia hesitated. "It looks like a home of bad spirits," she said.

Magda laughed. "Do not worry. If any spirits are in the house, they are happy." She led the way through the big door and up a flight of stairs.

Krysia followed, her eyes wide with wonder. Inside, Hull House was like a palace. There were oriental rugs on the floor and paintings on the walls. In a sunny room upstairs a table was laid out with paper, paints, and brushes. A gorgeous bouquet of red and white roses was set up by the window. "I see you have brought a friend today, Magda," a smiling woman said.

"This is Krysia," Magda said.

"Welcome, Krysia," the woman said gently. "You may call me Miss Jane. Would you like to paint a picture of the flowers?" She handed Krysia a brush.

A Surprise for Krysia (cont.)

Circle the correct answers.

• •

1. Magda and Krysia were from . . .

    a. Mexico.   b. China.   c. Poland.

2. Magda and Krysia were . . .

    a. poor.   b. rich.   c. old.

3. The name of the woman who started the Settlement House was . . .

    a. Susan.   b. Jane.   c. Ann.

4. One thing children could do at the Settlement House was . . .

    a. scrub floors.   b. study art.   c. cook.

5. The Settlement House was . . .

    a. a new building.   b. an old mansion.   c. an office tower.

6. The language Magda and Krysia spoke best was . . .

    a. English.   b. Polish.   c. Italian.

7. Their neighborhood was . . .

    a. almost deserted.   b. very rich.   c. very crowded .

8. When it rained, the streets were probably . . .

    a. muddy.   b. dry.   c. oily.

Name _____

Read the story. Use context clues to infer the meaning of the words in **bold**.

• •

Dylan waited on the playground in the shade of a big **cottonwood**. If the other members of the Mystery **Society** didn't show up soon, he would have to go meet the new **client** alone. Then, he saw Ryan and Madison running across the yard.

Ryan reached him first. "Sorry," he **gasped**. "We just got back from the field trip."

"Our bus had a flat tire," Madison added. She was bent over trying to catch her breath.

"Ok, well, we should get started," Dylan said. He led the way. "I got an e-mail this morning from a new boy in the neighborhood. He's in my little brother's class. He has a problem and he needs our help."

"Great!" said Madison. "We haven't had a case all month."

"Actually, we haven't had a case since last year," Ryan said.

Madison **shrugged**. "So, who's keeping track?"

Dylan stopped in front of a two-story house that had once been white. He pulled a piece of paper out of his pocket and checked the address. "This is it," he said.

The other two followed him up the **weed-choked** path to the door. Dylan knocked.

There was no answer at first, so he knocked again, harder. The big door opened slowly revealing a small boy in a red-striped T-shirt and jeans. "Are you the Mystery Society?" he asked.

"That's us! "I'm Dylan, and these are my **associates**, Ryan and Madison. May we come in?"

"Sure," said the boy. "I guess your brother Jack told you about me. I'm Joshua, but everybody calls me Josh." He led them to a small TV room and closed the door.

"What's the problem, Josh?" Dylan asked.

"I-I lost my grandfather's watch," Josh stammered. He looked as though he were going to cry. "If my mom finds out, I don't know what she'll do. It was worth a lot of money, and it was a family **heirloom**."

"It's ok, Josh. We'll help you find it," said Madison gently.

"When did you see it last?" asked Ryan.

Case of the Missing Heirloom (cont.)

Circle the correct answer.

• •

"I saw it the day after we moved. It was in the top drawer of my dresser. When I looked for it yesterday, it was gone," Josh said.

"Let's go take a look," said Dylan.

Josh took them upstairs to his room and pointed to the dresser. Dylan and Ryan asked Josh more questions. Madison took the top drawer all the way out. She reached into the space where the drawer had been. **Triumphant**, she pulled out the watch.

1. The word **triumphant** means . . .

    a. miserable.   b. disappointed.   c. victorious.

2. When Madison **shrugged** she moved her . . .

    a. shoulders.   b. head.   c. fingers.

3. A **cottonwood** is a . . .

    a. car.   b. tree.   c. animal.

4. An **heirloom** is . . .

    a. something inherited. b. a brush.   c. something to weave on.

5. A **client** is . . .

    a. a detective.   b. a student.   c. a customer.

6. A **society** is . . .

    a. a club.   b. a house.   c. a game.

7. If the path was **weed-choked**, the yard needed . . .

    a. some work.   b. a new fountain.   c. a dog.

8. The word **associates** means . . .

    a. enemies.   b. fellow workers.   c. students.

9. If you **gasp** you are trying to . . .

    a. pick up something.   b. catch your breath.   c. hold something.

Inferring • CD-104555

I Am Like a Forgotten Ruler

Read the poem. Use context clues to infer the answers to the questions on the next page.

I am like a forgotten ruler.
My personal tower
overlooks all
space and time.

I have a rodent
no cat can catch,
that guides a cursor
no knight can ride.

I fly to far lands
faster than the flick
of an eagle's eye.

My quick click
can capture
a terrible monster
within a frame,
and freeze it
as a hard rainbow
to hold in my hand.

I ride thin impulses
back to times
when Sumerians first
pressed stylus to clay.

From my tower
I gaze on cave horses
drawn before any city.
I look back on a star-like
Earth from dark space.

Linda Armstrong

I Am Like a Forgotten Ruler (cont.)

Circle the correct answers.

. . . .

1. This poem is a riddle. What is the tower?

   a. a castle
   b. a television transmission tower
   c. a computer

2. What is the "rodent no cat can catch"?

   a. a prairie dog
   b. a mouse
   c. a squirrel

3. When does this poem really take place?

   a. the past
   b. the present
   c. the future

4. What is the "hard rainbow" the speaker holds?

   a. a CD
   b. candy
   c. a scarf

5. How can the speaker look back at Earth from space?

   a. from a telescope
   b. from a tower
   c. from a web site

6. How does the speaker visit the cave paintings?

   a. on the Internet
   b. by flying to France
   c. by telepathy

7. What does the speaker think about the computer?

   a. hates it
   b. thinks it's great
   c. is afraid of it

Name _____

Harvest in Plymouth

Edward Winslow wrote a letter to a friend in 1621. In it, he describes the first Thanksgiving. Read the letter. Use context clues to infer the answers to the questions below.

. . . .

Last spring, we planted twenty acres of Indian corn and sowed some six acres of barley and peas. According to the manner of the American Indians, we fertilized our ground with fish. Our corn did well; and we had a good increase of Indian corn. Our barley grew fairly well, but our peas were not worth the gathering, for we feared they were too late sown. They came up very well, and blossomed; but the sun parched the blooms.

After the harvest, our governor sent four men to hunt wild fowl, so that we might, after a special manner, rejoice together after we had gathered the fruit of our labors. In one day, the four men gathered enough fowl to feed the company for almost a week. At which time, among other recreations, we practiced with our muskets. Many of the American Indians came among us, including their greatest king, Massasoit, with some ninety men, whom for three days we entertained and feasted. And they went out and gathered five deer, which they brought to the plantation, and bestowed on leaders.

We have a great abundance of fish and fowl. Our bay is full of lobsters all the summer and affords a variety of other fish. In September, we can take a barrel of eels in a night and can dig them out of their beds all the winter. All the springtime the earth sends forth naturally very good salad herbs. Here are red and white grapes, strawberries, gooseberries, raspberries, and three kinds of plums.

1. Why does the corn grow well? _____

2. Was beef or lamb served at the feast? Why or why not? _____

    _____

3. The American Indians have no written records of the celebration. Do you believe it was an important event in their lives? Why or why not? _____

    _____

4. From the letter, what do you think they served at the feast? _____

    _____

    Which food did they definitely not have at the feast? _____

    _____

Answer Key

Page 4
Answers vary. Examples:
1. autumn; Pumpkins are an autumn vegetable. 2. no; He did not have a pie. 3. large; Speaker huffed while carrying it. 4. Answers vary.

Page 5
Answers vary. Examples:
1. teacher/school nurse; She must call the school for a sick day. 2. no; He painted on the spots. 3. David will get in trouble.

Page 6
Answers vary. Examples:
1. girl; Quinn is called a "she." 2. doctor; She worked late to help sick patients. 3. Mom fell asleep on the couch. 4. night; It's late. 5. He goes back to sleep. The house is full of snores.

Pages 7–8
Answers vary. Examples:
1. They do not like it. 2. It is the first day of school. 3. brothers; 4. morning; 5. He is brushing his teeth. 6. sixth; 7. excited; nervous; 8. breakfast

Page 9
1. writing; Debbie is thanking her for her letter. 2. pool; lying on the deck, going to take a dip; 3. jelly; It goes with peanut butter.

Page 10
1. B; 2. C; 3. B; 4. A; 5. C; tiny

Pages 11–12
Circle: 1. studied; confident; was prepared; 3. did not study; nervous; was not prepared Write: 2. an A+; 4. a bad grade

Page 13
1. stamp; 2. magnet; 3. Band-Aid; 4. star; 5. light bulb; 6. lightning

Page 14
Answers vary. Examples:
1. to earn money for tickets; 2. to buy tickets with the money she earned; 3. an autograph

Pages 15–16
Circle: 1. B; 2. A; 3. B; 4. B; 5. A
Write: 1. Mr. Chan tells them to quiet down and go back to their desks. 2. She is eager. 3. A fire truck comes; there is smoke. 4. They carry a hose to the part of the building that is smoking. 5. The fire is in the cafeteria.

Pages 17–18
Answers vary. Examples:
1. excited; He jumps up and down. 2. probably; He was the star batter. 3. nervous; His batting average has gone down. 4. yes; He hit the winning home run. 5. relaxed; She never gets butterflies in her stomach. 6. yes; She kept her cool even when they were losing.

Page 19
Answers vary.

Pages 20–21
Circle: 1. B; 2. C; 3. A; 4. B; 5. A; 6. C; 7. A

Pages 22–23
Circle: 1. B; Write: 2. yes; It will rain and the wind will blow the dust away. 3. Answers will vary.

Page 24
Answers vary. Examples: 1. It was taken out with the trash. 2. The can was empty and the garbage truck drove down the street. 3. The garbage collectors. 4. The backpack smelled like garbage. 5. Unhappy

Pages 25–26
1. yes; She's an amateur and she is not prepared. 2. no; She does not even have dance shoes. 3. nervous; Her stomach twists. 4. yes; She was asked to continue singing because a man In the audience liked her voice.

Pages 27–28
1. windy and snowy; 2. cold and clear; 3. cool and clear; 4. cold and clear; 5. cool and clear; 6. cool and rainy

Page 29
Answers vary. Examples: 1. Civil War; 2. there are soldiers; 3. slavery

Pages 30–31
1. 1492; 2. Christopher Columbus; He is captaining three ships headed for the Indies. 3. They had not made port to get fresh food in a long time. 4. small; 5. the Americas; 6. Answers vary.

Page 32
Answers vary. Examples: 1. plaintiff; 2. Zachary did not make a convincing argument. 3. He said his uncle from NASA gave him the pen, and the pen said NASA on its side. 4. happy because he won the trial; grumpy because he lost the trial

Page 33
Answers vary. Examples: 1. a nestling; Umberto had to place it back in a nest. 2. no; Umberto did not take it to the rehabilitation center. 3. yes; Umberto was satisfied when he checked the nest.

Pages 34–35
Circle: 1. A; 2. A; 3. B; 4. B; 5. C; 6. B; 7. C; 8. B; 9. A

Page 36
Circle: 1. C; 3. C; Write: 2. at the department of motor vehicles; to get his driver's license; a. He asks for the car keys. b. He calls himself a driver. c. The sign says he has to be 16 to get a license. 4. car keys; 5. gas tank; 6. excited because he passed the test

Page 37
Answers vary. Examples: 1. Elephants would have been extinct. Their numbers were decreasing. 2. The elephant population will go back up. Humans do not bother them to get ivory any more.

Page 38
I. library; 2. submarine; 3. outer space; 4. cave; 5. rainforest; 6. train

Pages 39-40
Circle: I. C; 2. A; 3. B; 4. B; 5. B; 6. B; 7. C; 8. A

Pages 41-42
Circle: I. C; 2. A; 3. B; 4. A; 5. C; 6. A; 7. A; 8. B; 9. B

Pages 43-44
Circle: I. C; 2. B; 3. B; 4. A; 5. C; 6. A; 7. B

Page 45
Answers vary. Examples: I. They fertilize it with fish. 2. no; They do not have cows or sheep. 3. yes; They were eating with new people, and they sent their greatest king. 4. They served corn, berries, and fowl. They did not serve peas.

Inferring • CD-104555